I'd Scream Except I Look So Fabulous

Other Cathy® Books from Andrews McMeel Publishing

I Am Woman, Hear Me Snore
Abs of Steel, Buns of Cinnamon
Understanding the "Why" Chromosome
The Child Within Has Been Awakened But the Old Lady on the Outside Just Collapsed
Revelations from a 45-Pound Purse
Only Love Can Break a Heart, But a Shoe Sale Can Come Close
$14 in the Bank and a $200 Face in My Purse
My Granddaughter Has Fleas!!
Why Do the Right Words Always Come Out of the Wrong Mouth?
A Hand to Hold, an Opinion to Reject
Thin Thighs in Thirty Years
Wake Me Up When I'm a Size 5
Men Should Come with Instruction Booklets
A Mouthful of Breath Mints and No One to Kiss
Another Saturday Night of Wild and Reckless Abandon

Cathy Twentieth Anniversary Collection
Reflections: A Fifteenth Anniversary Collection

———————————————————

Confessions to My Mother
Girl Food: Cathy's Cookbook for the Well-Balanced Woman

I'd Scream Except I Look So Fabulous

A *Cathy®* Collection by Cathy Guisewite

**Andrews McMeel
Publishing**

Kansas City

Cathy® may be viewed on the Internet at:
www.uexpress.com

5

Panel 1:
WHAT HAPPENED TO THE NEW TAX LAWS? EVERYTHING WAS GOING TO BE DIFFERENT THIS YEAR.

YOU WERE GOING TO BE DIFFERENT THIS YEAR, TOO, CATHY.

Panel 2:
BUT TAX REFORMS WERE PASSED! THINGS WERE SUPPOSED TO BE DIFFERENT!

YOU REFORMED, TOO, AND YOU'RE NOT DIFFERENT.

Panel 3:
IF IT TAKES ONE OF YOU THIS LONG TO BE DIFFERENT, MULTIPLY YOURSELF OUT AND IMAGINE HOW LONG IT WOULD TAKE FOR A WHOLE BUNCH OF YOU TO BE DIFFERENT!

Panel 4:
NEXT YEAR I'M GOING TO HAVE A DIFFERENT ACCOUNTANT.

IT'S SO TOUCHING TO HEAR THEM DREAM.

Panel 5:
YOUR TOTAL 1996 TAXES ARE...

AACK! MY HEART! MY CHEST!

TAX WORK BOOK

ACCOUNTANT

Panel 6:
MY LUNGS! I CAN'T BREATHE! MY THROAT IS CLOSING! MY PULSE HAS STOPPED! ALSO, I'M BLIND! HELP! SOMEONE HELP!!

Panel 7:
SPLAT.

ACCOUNTANT

Panel 8:
MY JOB: PART C.P.A., PART C.P.R.

ACCOUNTANT

Panel 9:
THE IRS CANCELED "CYBER-FILE," A PROGRAM TO LET PEOPLE FILE FROM THEIR HOME COMPUTERS, BECAUSE OF TECHNOLOGICAL GLITCHES AND BUNGLED SECURITY.

HA, HA, HA!

Panel 10:
I KNEW YOU'D BE PLEASED. ALL OF YOUR 1996 TAXES WENT TO INVESTIGATE WHY THE IRS PAID $1099.00 EACH FOR CELL PHONES FOR "CYBER-FILE" PERSONNEL WHEN WE ALL KNOW FROM NEWSPAPER ADS THAT YOU CAN GET CELL PHONES FOR FREE!

Panel 11:
YOUR TAX DOLLARS HELPED SHUT DOWN A SYSTEM THAT WHO-KNOWS-HOW-MANY MILLIONS OF PREVIOUS TAX DOLLARS WERE FLUSHED DOWN AN OVERPRICED TOILET TO DEVELOP!!

Panel 12:
PBLTTT!

BLOW YOUR NOSE IN AS MANY IRS FORMS AS YOU WANT. YOU'RE PAYING FOR THE STAPLES THIS YEAR.

ACCOUNTANT

11

14

16

19

25

31

THE HOME OFFICE: DAY 1

TO SET UP | TO CALL | TO WRITE | TO READ | TO ORDER | TO LEARN | TO FILE | TO EAT

32

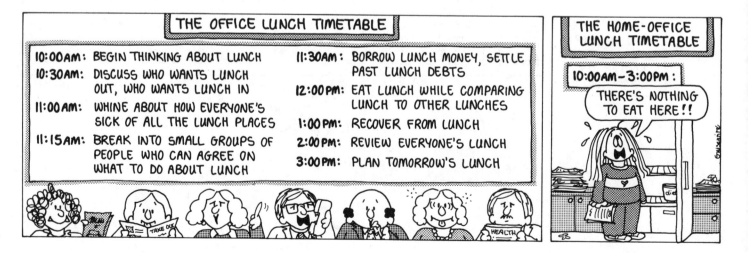

35

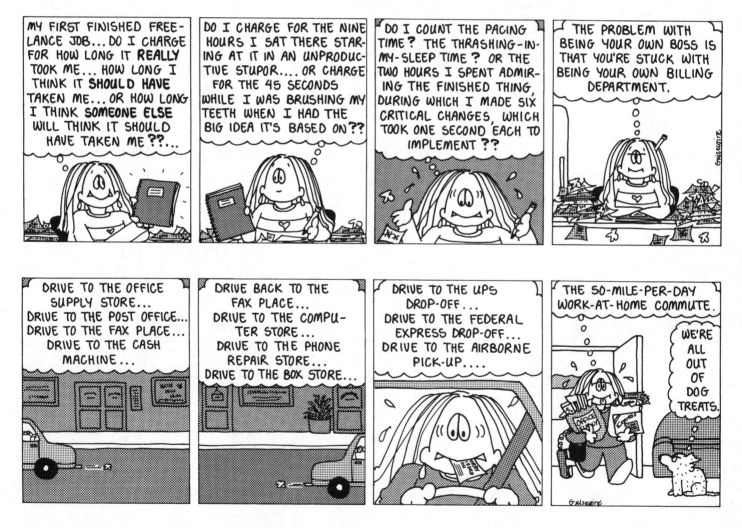

40

41

Panel 1:
I WROTE A LIST OF BUSINESS LEADS FOR YOU, CATHY.

NO! THE DISGUST I HAVE FOR YOU IS SO PURE RIGHT NOW! DON'T RUIN IT BY BEING NICE!

Panel 2:
IT'S HARD TO MAKE COLD CALLS, SO I SPOKE TO EACH OF THEM ON YOUR BEHALF.

IT TOOK ME SO LONG TO BE COMPLETELY REPULSED! DON'T DO IT! DON'T ENDEAR YOURSELF!!

Panel 3:
THEY'RE ALL ANXIOUS TO HEAR FROM YOU!

AACK! I FEEL GRATEFULNESS CREEPING IN! I SENSE FONDNESS! IT'S GETTING ALL MURKY AGAIN!!!

Panel 4:
SOME SEE THE WORLD IN BLACK AND WHITE. I GET SPECTRA-CONFUSION.

Panel 5:
BYE, ELECTRA...KISS, KISS....IT WAS SO GOOD TO SEE YOU AGAIN...KISS, KISS.

Panel 6:
YOU'RE SUCH A BEAUTIFUL GIRL... SUCH A WONDERFUL SWEETHEART...KISS KISS... I LOVE YOU SO MUCH...YES I DO... ...KISS..KISS..KISS...

Panel 7:
SEE YOU, CATHY.

SEE YOU, IRVING.

Panel 8:
WHICH IS WORSE: THE MOMENT YOU REALIZE A MAN ISN'T CAPABLE OF LOVE...OR THE MOMENT YOU REALIZE HE IS.

Panel 9:
...WHEW! IRVING'S GONE, ELECTRA! NOW WE CAN GET BACK TO...

Panel 10:
...YOUR HAIR SMELLS LIKE IRVING'S AFTERSHAVE! I TOLD YOU NOT TO PLAY WITH HIM! NOW YOU'RE COVERED WITH HIS SCENT!

Panel 11:
I SPENT THREE YEARS GETTING THAT SCENT OUT OF MY MIND! I FUMIGATED MY BRAIN! I REFUSE TO BE HAUNTED BY THAT SCENT AGAIN!!

Panel 12:

HUMANS AND THEIR NOSES...

42

43

Panel 1: HI, CATHY. HOW'S IT GOING? / I CAN'T COMPLAIN, CHARLENE.

Panel 2: ...ACTUALLY, I **CAN** COMPLAIN, BUT I SHOULDN'T COMPLAIN... ACTUALLY, I **SHOULD** COMPLAIN, BUT I WON'T COMPLAIN... ACTUALLY, I **WOULD** COMPLAIN, BUT I **COULDN'T** COM... WAIT. DID I ALREADY DO THAT ONE??

Panel 3: ...WAIT! JUST KEEP TALKING! JUST STAY ON THE LINE WITH ME!!

Panel 4: HOW'S SHE DOING? / TOO MUCH TIME IN A ROOM BY HERSELF. / WHAT WAS THE QUESTION?

Panel 5: MR. PINKLEY DESPERATELY NEEDS YOU TO HELP MAKE A PRESENTATION THIS WEEK, CATHY. / HE NEEDS ME?

Panel 6: PHIL CAN'T DO IT BECAUSE HE'S ON VACATION... TED WON'T DO IT BECAUSE HE'S TICKED AT PHIL...

Panel 7: JAN WON'T DO IT BECAUSE SHE THINKS TED'S A BABY... MARK WON'T DO IT BECAUSE JAN THREW OUT HIS JALAPENO DIP WHEN SHE FUMIGATED THE REFRIGERATOR...

Panel 8: YOU'RE THE ONLY ONE WE KNOW WHO ISN'T TANGLED UP IN THE INTRA-OFFICE-PETTY-BICKERING LOOP. / AT LAST. INDISPENSABILITY.

Panel 9: IT'S YOUR FIRST MEETING IN YOUR OLD OFFICE SINCE YOU WERE OUTSOURCED. YOU CAN DO IT!

Panel 10: BE BRIGHT! BE CONFIDENT! BE OPEN! BE INTERESTING! MESMERIZE THEM WITH YOUR UNIQUE BLEND OF STRENGTH AND ACCESSIBILITY!!

Panel 11: MAINTAIN THE ATTITUDE FOR EXACTLY TWO HOURS... THEN BOLT FOR HOME, LOCK THE DOOR, THROW ON A SWEATSUIT AND RESUME LIFE! / PRODUCT TESTING, INC.

Panel 12: SOONER OR LATER, WE ALL USE OUR DIPLOMA FROM THE BLIND DATE SCHOOL OF LIFE.

50

53

Panel 1: IF I'D MADE ALBUMS AS LIFE WENT ALONG, ALL THESE PICTURES OF IRVING AND ALEX WOULD BE IN THEM...

Panel 2: ...BUT I'M DOING THE ALBUMS NOW. DO I PUT IRVING AND ALEX IN THEM AND ENSHRINE OUR FAILED RELATIONSHIPS AS AN HONEST PART OF MY PAST?

Panel 3: ...OR DO I DUMP THEM AND OBLITERATE THEM FROM THE RECORD?

DUMP THEM! PRETEND THEY NEVER HAPPENED! DUMP THEM ALL!!

Panel 4: VERY SENTIMENTAL...

HOW MANY MOMENTS OF PERSONAL POWER DOES THE MOTHER OF A GROWN-UP GET?

Panel 5: WORKING ON YOUR PHOTO ALBUMS INSPIRED ME TO FINISH MINE, CATHY!

YOU FINISHED, MOM??

Panel 6: NO, BUT I'M GETTING THERE! YOUR BABY BOOK IS ASSEMBLED...MOST OF OUR CHRISTMAS PICTURES HAVE BEEN FOUND...THE '80s ARE BASICALLY IN CHRONOLOGICAL ORDER...

Panel 7: I CAN FINALLY SEE THE ...**AAACK!!**

...MOM???

Panel 8: I SAW THE LIGHT AT THE END OF THE TUNNEL, AND IT WAS SHINING ON A CARTON OF UNLABELED SLIDES, HOME MOVIES AND VIDEOS!!

MISC. SLIDES MOVIES VIDEOS

BOX #1

Panel 9: MAYBE YOU'LL MEET SOMEONE AT ONE OF THE NEW COMPANIES YOU'RE FREELANCING FOR, CATHY!

I DON'T WANT TO MEET ANYONE RIGHT NOW, MOM.

Panel 10: WHY NOT? YOU'RE YOUNG! YOU SHOULD BE GETTING OUT!

I'M SICK OF MEETING MEN!

Panel 11: YOU'RE SO PRETTY! SO SMART! YOU HAVE SO MUCH TO OFFER!

I'M SICK OF MEETING THEM, SICK OF GETTING TO KNOW THEM...SICK OF THEM ALL!!!

Panel 12: I FEEL LIKE A POM-POM GIRL FOR A TEAM THAT'S DECIDED TO SIT OUT THE SEASON.

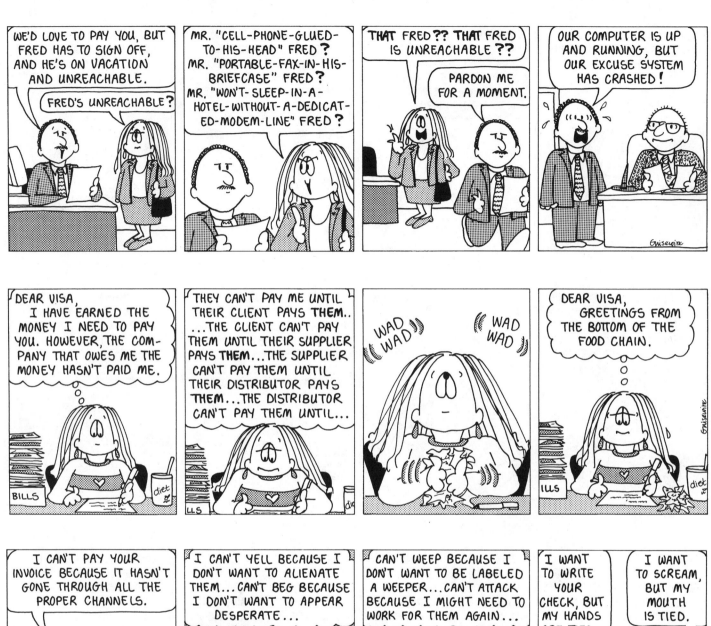

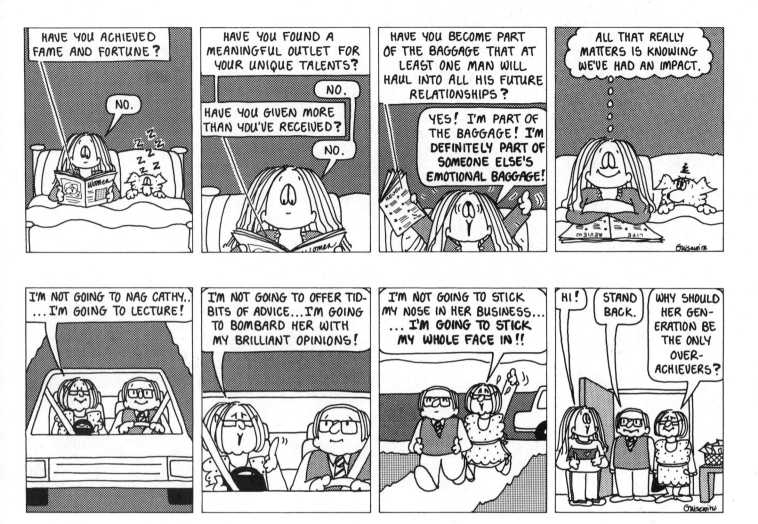

66

71

74

79

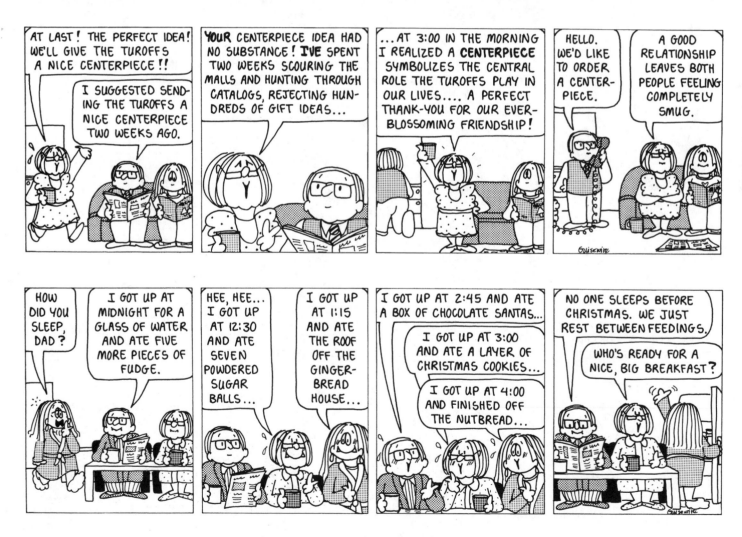

95

97

102

107

110

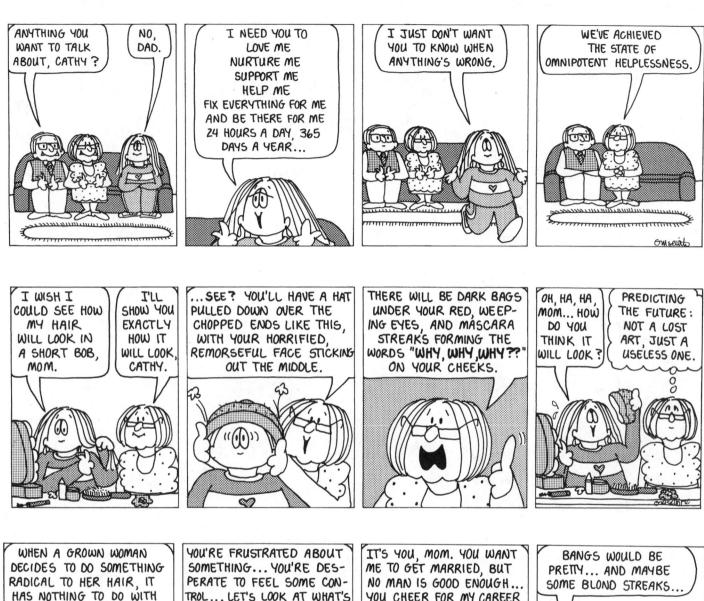

125

126

Gift

JUN 0 8 2010